MacOS Ventura

SENIORS GUIDE

2023

A Step-by-Step Manual for the Non-Tech-Savvy
to Master to the Most Updated Apple's Desktop Operating
System

John Halbert

Contents

INTRODUCTION

macOS Ventura is the latest version of the macOS, which is the operating system that runs on Apple's Mac computers. This update is significant as it introduces a multitasking experience and adds new capabilities across the platform. This may all sound complicated to grasp, so let's start with the basics before mastering this updated operating system.

Mac is a nickname (abbreviation) given to the Macintosh line of computers made by Apple Inc., and they come in a variety of models with the most common being the iMac that has the computer built into the screen monitor.

Their competitors are the PCs operating on Microsoft's operating system called Windows. Although Macs are generally capable of running the same functions as a Window's PC, such as accessing the internet, word processing, and playing media, among others, most of these features require different programs than those common on a PC.

With that said, Macs have quite a few advantages over PCs. For one, they are known for the quality of their build and are considered much easier to use than their Windows counterpart. They also have fewer hardware incompatibilities in comparison to PCs as the Macs are exclusively made by Apple and do not have other manufacturers, unlike Microsoft, which licenses Windows to third-party computer makers. It is also worth noting that they are much more protected against computer viruses.

The thing that makes Macs different from other computers is the operating system that powers them. macOS is designed specifically for the hardware it runs on, letting you do things that would otherwise prove to be challenging on other computers. It comes with a suite of powerful apps designed to perform various functions. It ensures that all your photos, documents, and other important stuff are kept up to date on all your other Apple devices and you don't need to worry about privacy and security as there are strong features in place to ensure data security.

This leads us to circle back to macOS Ventura. As previously mentioned, this is the latest version of the Mac Operating System. It is the 13th version of Mac's Operating System, and with every update, there are always going to be new features introduced with the aim of creating a new experience for the users. macOS Ventura is no different and, in this book, we are going to discuss all the ways in which you can successfully master the most updated Apple Desktop Operating System in simple steps.

PART ONE: A BEGINNER'S GUIDE TO USING A MAC

Overview

In order to understand the latest Mac Operating System and ways in which it eases access, it is very important to first understand the basics of a Mac computer.

Learning the basics of Mac is not a difficult task. This is especially true if you are transitioning from a Windows PC. Although the two are quite different—by a mile—it does help to have some knowledge of the latter, but it's not necessary.

For decades, Microsoft Windows has been the dominant operating system and is still very popular as it has a leg up on its Apple counterparts. However, despite dominating at least 87% of the markets, they face overwhelming competition with the Macs as more people adopt Apple gadgets into their daily lives.

The biggest disparity between the two dominating companies is that Microsoft licenses Windows to computer makers but Apple does not sell macOS to anyone. Their operating system runs on the computers Apple itself makes, and while this factor makes their products a tad bit expensive to purchase when compared to others in the market, it's for this very reason that makes them the best in compatibility. In comparison to Windows PCs, macOS is much less likely to have compatibility problems because it's software and peripherals only need to work with a small set of computers.

If you are coming here from a Windows PC, then you're probably used to the start menu. That is the first thing you see on your PC when you power it, and the start menu eases access to the features on your computer. However, there is no start menu in macOS. Another thing you might be accustomed to with Windows PC, is the shortcuts accessed by simply using the Ctrl key on the keyboard. While Mac keyboards have Ctrl keys on them, they do not carry the same function as Windows. Most Mac keyboard shortcuts can be accessed by using Command (CMD), which will have either a picture of a clover leaf or an Apple.

Despite their stark differences, some of the basics between the two are quite similar. For example, the two are window-based graphic user interfaces (GUIs) that are operated by a mouse and keyboard. Some features like double-clicking to open things and a trash bin for deleted files are similar.

We are not going to focus on how different Windows PCs and macOS are, but on the key elements, you need to learn to ensure you're well-equipped to adapt to the Mac. It may all sound confusing at first but, in this chapter, we are going to cover all the basics you need to learn to get started with the Mac and ease your experience in navigating its operating system.

Navigating macOS

The Dock

This is a set of shortcuts to the apps installed on your Mac, and it runs along the bottom of the screen. Any app that comes with the Mac or you install yourself can be found in this section. You can also drag icons on the dock to create shortcuts and drag them off if you need to delete the shortcuts.

You can rearrange apps on the dock in an order that suits you. To see more options, you simply right-click the dock icons.

The Spotlight

This is the search function on your macOS. You can access this function by either clicking the magnifying glass icon located at the top right of your screen or pressing Command (CMD) + Space.

By clicking this icon, you will not only be able to search for items within your Mac but also look for things on the internet as well as the App Store. As you start typing in the spotlight search window, it will give you suggestions as to what you are looking for and you can simply click on them instead of typing the entire thing, thus saving you time.

The Menu Bar

The menu bar is located at the top of your screen and it can change depending on the app you are currently working on. Say, for example. you're using Mail, the options and setting you'll see are for Mail.

However, if you look to the far left of the screen, you'll see an Apple icon that stays the same no matter what app you are using. This icon offers system shortcuts and access to shut down, restart. or log out options.

If you need to access your notifications and settings, including those to Wi-Fi, date, and time reset, then you will find them on the right side of the menu bar.

The App Store

This is a feature you will find on your iPhone but you don't necessarily need to use it on the Mac. Apple controls the apps you can install onto your device by restricting some apps from the App Store.

However, this isn't necessarily a bad thing. By controlling the apps you can access, they reduce the risk of downloading something that may contain malware. If you still want to access an app absent in the store, you can download it from anywhere; you just need to be careful about where you decide to download it from.

The Activity Monitor

To access this, you can simply open it via Spotlight, but essentially, it's located under utilities, which is under applications.

If you are coming from Windows, it's like the task manager where you can find your memory, energy, disk, CPU, and network information. On some occasions, where you're having problems with certain apps, you can use the activity monitor to select processes and force them to stop.

Safari

Safari is a web browser, making its functions different from those of Spotlight's.

It allows Apple users to browse the web and it contains everything you would expect from any other web browser you may have previously used. However, if you are used to a certain browser and would prefer to stick to it, then you can use some of the popular browsers like Chrome on your macOS.

Ask Siri

This is Apple's voice assistant, a feature also present on the iPhone. The Siri icon is found in the top right section of your menu bar but you can easily access it by pressing and holding Cmd + Space.

You can use this voice assistant to do anything from searching for things on the internet to opening different apps and even setting up a meeting for you.

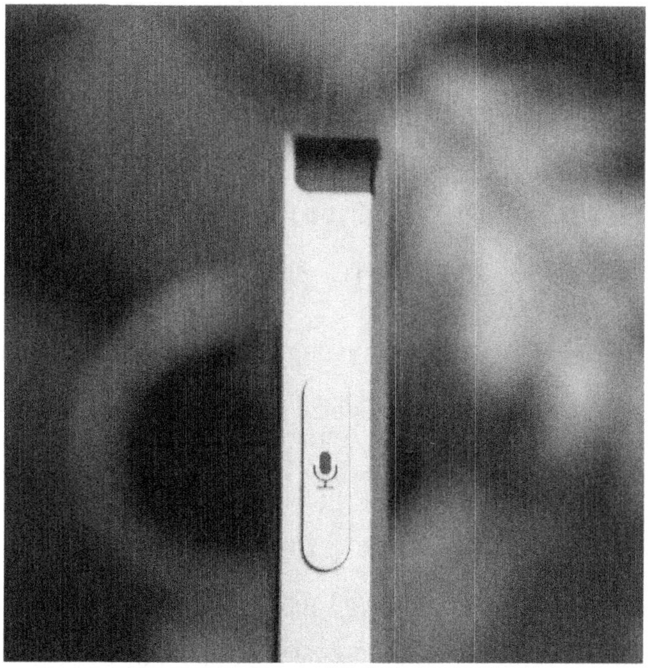

How to Enable Siri

To access Siri on your Mac, you need to select the "System setting" which is under the Apple Menu, and then click "Siri and Spotlight" in the sidebar. If you can't immediately see it, you may need to scroll down.

Apple Menu > System Settings > Siri and Spotlight

The second step is turning on Siri if it's not already on and then click "Enable." You cannot use Siri if you are not connected to the internet, so you need to ensure that it's on.

You may be asked if you want to improve Siri and dictation, and if you do, then you can either share audio recordings by clicking "Share Audio Recordings" which essentially enables Apple to store the audio of your Siri and Dictation interaction from your Mac or you can choose to not share your audio by clicking "Not now."

However, in case you go with the first option but change your mind later, you can stop the audio recordings by opening "System setting" under the Apple Menu and then clicking on "Privacy and Security" in the sidebar. You then scroll to "Analytics and Improvements" and from here, you can adjust the settings on your Siri and Dictations by turning them on or off.

Apple Menu > System Settings > Privacy & Security > Analytics & Improvements

How to Use Siri

You need to turn on listen for "Hey Siri" and if you turn on "Allow Siri when locked," then you can use the voice assistant even when your Mac is in sleep mode or locked.

To choose how Siri speaks, click on the language pop-up menu and choose your preferred language from the present options. You can get a preview of how the voice assistant sounds by clicking select next to "Siri voice" before finally settling on the voice you want from the options presented to you.

If you need to mute Siri, click on Siri responses and turn off "voice feedback." This way, you get a display of Siri's response in the Siri window with the voice muted.

To display what either you or Siri say on the screen, you click Siri responses then turn on "Always show Siri captions" for Siri's response and "Always show speech" for your response.

You can ease access to Siri by adding it to the Menu bar and, to do this, select "System Settings" under the Apple Menu and then click "Control center" in the sidebar. Next, go to the Menu Bar on the right and choose "Show in menu bar" next to Siri.

Apple Menu > System Settings > Control Center

Apps

To access the apps on your macOS, you will find them stored in the "Application Folder" which, unlike Windows, does not contain other folders. While some apps may need other files to run, macOS apps are usually self-contained and are represented by a single icon that you can run by simply double-clicking.

System Preferences

If you are familiar with Windows, then the System Preferences is the control panel of macOS. If not, then this is basically where you access the setting and controls for how your Mac runs.

You can access System Preferences by either clicking on the Apple icon in your menu bar or even using Spotlight to search for that option.

There are quite a number of changes you can make to your Mac by accessing this feature, some of which include your display, network settings, printer, and Bluetooth, among others. However, it's important to not make any changes to items you are unfamiliar with.

Setting Up a New Mac

Once you are done navigating through the features present on your Mac, you can take additional steps to ease access.

Set Up the Internet

There are various ways to go about this. You can either use an ethernet cable by plugging it into your Mac to connect to the internet or use Wi-Fi if you are within the range of a Wi-Fi network.

How to Connect to the Wi-Fi

If you are using a public Wi-Fi network, you can connect to the connection by clicking the Wi-Fi icon in the menu bar and selecting the network you want to join. You may be asked to enter a password for the network before joining and you can use that to access the network.

To join a hidden Wi-Fi network, you first need to know the name of the network, its security protocol, and the password.

To access it, click the Wi-Fi icon in the menu bar of your Mac, click on other networks, and then click "other" at the bottom of the list. You'll then be presented with a type bar where you are required to enter the name of the wireless network in the network name field. You'll need to then click the security pop-up menu and then choose the type of wireless security the network uses. The next step will require you to enter information such as username and password, or any additional information that may be displayed, then you can click "join" to access the network.

Change Scroll Direction

It's possible to change the direction of your scroll if it's in the opposite direction you'd prefer it to be. To go about this, you need to "Select Preferences" and then click on the mouse and you can adjust the scroll direction by selecting "Natural."

Apple Menu > System Preferences > Mouse

Visual Customization

You can make adjustments to the look of the macOS by making changes to the desktop background, log-in image, screen saver, or the color of certain elements by accessing them in System Preferences.

To switch between light and dark mode or adjust the brightness of your screen, you'll also find these settings under System Preferences.

If you want to change the wallpaper displayed on your desktop, you can either choose from a variety of pictures provided by Apple or one of your own. One of the easiest ways to go about this is by dragging the image from a folder and onto the thumbnail of the current desktop picture to use as your profile image.

Set Up Your Printer

If your printer is already connected to your network, then it's going to be easy to connect it to your Mac. To achieve this, under "System Preferences," select the "Printers and Scanners" option. Click the plus button and your macOS should automatically connect to your printer.

If you decide to connect the two via USB, then you're going to first plug your printer's USB into your desktop. Click the Apple icon and select "System Preferences" then click on "Printers and Scanners." Click the plus (+) sign below the "List of printers" and click "Add" to the printer you've selected.

Set Up Backups

Time Machine is a backup software included in macOS and it's set to automatically back up your files. This eases access to your files or apps in case something goes wrong and you accidentally lose them; you can reinstall them exactly how they were.

Time Machine will make your experience easier as you are certain of recovering your information especially when you are a first-time user and just getting a hang of things.

Add Users

If you plan to share your Mac with someone else, then you can add new users by accessing "Users and Groups" which is under System Preferences. You can even set up guest users and change your user password here.

In case you are worried that adding a user to your Mac is going to affect the apps or settings you have made, then you don't have to be. There will be two different accounts and you'll each be able to use your apps and settings without affecting the other user.

Install Cyber Security

Although macOS is known for its stellar security, recent years have seen the emergence of malware for macOS more than before. It's important to install a good security app that offers on-demand scans and real-time protection.

Set Up Security Codes or Fingerprints

You can use the touch ID on your Mac or magic keyboard to unlock it, authorize purchases from the App Store or Apple Books on the web using Apple Pay, or even sign-in into some third-party apps. To do this, you need to set it up first.

How to Set Up Touch ID

If your Mac or magic keyboard has a touch ID, you'll find the sensor at the top right of your keyboard.

To access the touch ID, you need to select the system setting which is under the Apple Menu. Click the "Touch ID and Password" in the sidebar. Add "fingerprint" and then enter your password following which your screen will light up with additional instructions.

Apple Menu > System Settings > Touch ID and Password > Add Fingerprint

You are allowed to add up to three fingerprints to your user account but you can save up to five fingerprints on your Mac if you're sharing it with another user.

How to Use the Touch ID

You can use your Touch ID to unlock your Mac when you must wake it from sleep mode or when you need to access a password-protected app.

You can also use it for Apple Pay to complete any purchases you make on your Mac. These purchases may include ones made on the iTunes store, Apple Books, or the App Store. To do this, log in to your Mac using your password, purchase the item from any of the stores, and then place your finger on the Touch ID when asked.

Touch ID can also be used to automatically fill in user names, passwords, credit card information, and other sensitive information when requested while using apps such as Safari.

It can also be used to switch between user accounts on the Mac and to do this, you need to set up fast user switchin, in which case, the user you switch to must have already logged into the Mac by entering a password. To make the switch, click the fast user switching menu in the menu bar and choose a different user, then place your finger on the Touch ID.

You need to be logged in with your password in order to be able to use Touch ID for all the listed tasks. You also need to note that the only accounts that can be accessed by Touch ID are the user account and not guest users or sharing-only users.

How to Delete Fingerprints

To delete or rename fingerprints, select the "System Settings" under the Apple Menu, then click "Touch ID and Passwords" in the sidebar.

To rename the fingerprint, click the text below a fingerprint and enter the name you would like to replace it with.

To delete a fingerprint, select the particular fingerprint you want to remove, enter your password and then click delete.

How to Fix Problems with Touch ID

One of the most common issues associated with this is when the Touch ID does not recognize your fingerprint. This is not a matter that should worry you and the first thing you need to do is ensure that your finger is clean and dry. Cuts on the skin and moisture can affect fingerprint recognition.

If your Mac still requests a password after using Touch ID, it doesn't mean that it's broken. Some of the reasons for this may include having five incorrect fingerprint attempts in which case you will be asked for a password. You're also going to be required to enter a password every 48 hours.

In case you are worried that the individual you are sharing the Mac with will make changes to the setting of your fingerprint identification, then you shouldn't be. The security measures on the macOS ensure that only logged-in users can access their own touch ID information and not even the administrator can change the other user's fingerprint settings.

Create Apple ID

You need to have an Apple ID to be able to access all Apple services like iCloud, iMessage, and Music, among others. The ID consists of an email address and a password. The email address should look something like 'john_mark1@icloud.com'. Depending on where you reside, you may have the option to use a phone number instead of an email address as your Apple ID.

It is recommended that you use the same Apple ID for all Apple services.

To create an Apple ID on your Mac, you can use your current email address if you have one already or have an iCloud email address generated for you. To do this, select "System Settings" under the Apple Menu, then click "sign in with your Apple ID" at the top of the sidebar.

Click the "Create Apple ID" option at the top of the sidebar and then follow the onscreen instructions.

Apple Menu > System Settings > Sign in with Apple ID > Create ID

It is important not to share your Apple ID and password with anyone to ensure that your access to Apple services and any purchases you make are secure.

However, if you want to include your family members and share your purchases with them, you can set up a Family Sharing group of up to five people.

In purchase sharing, one person pays for everyone's purchases. How this happens is everyone in your family will have access to books, apps, music, and T.V. shows you purchase. To go about this, you're going to have to set up Family Sharing in macOS Ventura.

Open the Apple Menu and select "Systems Sharing" and then click "Family." If you don't see this option, tap your name and it will direct you to "Family Sharing" and then turn on "Share my purchases."

If you want to see what payment method to be billed, click on "Purchase Sharing" and look at the shared payment method information.

Easy Tips and Tricks for Using Mac

Learning essential tips can help streamline your experience and make the most out of your computer, especially if you are a new user.

Force Apps to Quit

Force quit is a useful tool for when an app is slowing down your Mac or refusing to close.

As previously discussed, you can force quit Mac apps from the Activity monitor, however, to ease access to the feature and open the "force quit application" tool, press Cmd + Opt +Esc and select the app and click "force quit." Of course, you will be asked to confirm if you want to quit and, in this case, you will be given the option to either "cancel" or proceed to "Force quit."

Save Battery

Everyone wants their batteries to last for as long as possible and it's important to sort out your battery use. To do this, head to "System Preferences" and select the "Energy saver" option to manage how long it should take for your Mac to go to sleep when idle.

Find the Cursor

Sometimes you may have a lot going on the screen and fail to see where your cursor is currently at. The easiest way to go about this is by moving your mouse around; doing so makes it easier to track the cursor.

Auto Unlock with Apple Watch

If you own an Apple Watch, you can set your Mac to automatically unlock whenever the two devices are near each other. What this does is save you time from having to type in your password to unlock your Mac. Additionally, you can use your Apple Watch to approve other password requests in macOS.

Troubleshooting Your Mac

You should expect your Mac to run properly, especially when you first purchase it. However, the Mac isn't exactly immune to problems, so you may run into some common issues, and when you do, here are a few ways you could go about solving them.

If Your Mac can't Turn On

Your Mac should be able to turn on without any issues but in the event this happens, don't panic. Here are some steps you can take to fix the problem.

Steps to Take

Check your power connections. If the power cable is not securely plugged into your Mac or is damaged, then your Mac will not turn on. You also need to ensure that the electric outlet is not faulty.

Press and hold the power button. Every Mac has a power button and you'll need to press it for about 10 seconds and then release it.

Unplug accessories, including printers, USB hubs, drives, and mobile devices, and then press and hold the power button to turn it on. An issue from an accessory could be the source of the problem, so you need to unplug all of them to confirm that is indeed the problem.

If you see something on your screen, say a prohibitory circle with a line through it, then it means your Mac contains an incompatible operating system that is a different version or build from that which your Mac can use. To fix this, you'll need to turn off your Mac and use disk utility to repair your startup disk.

If you're Mac still doesn't turn on after running all the basic troubleshooting, then it's important to contact the Apple support team for assistance.

Mac Freeze-ups

Say you are right in the middle of doing something and suddenly your Mac freezes up and the system stops responding. That can be a tad frustrating, but don't be tempted to swipe it off the table and onto the floor. Sometimes you may find your mouse cursor moving but instead of an arrow, you see a spinning ball, thus making it hard for you to carry on with what you were doing.

There are many reasons this could happen but the most common one is overloading the processor. Viruses and malware can also cause your Mac to freeze, so it's recommended to run a full virus scan to check if that's what causing the freeze.

How to Unfreeze Your Mac

Force quit is a tool that can be used to unfreeze your Mac. This can give you control over your frozen Mac when it's unresponsive and you can open it via keyboard shortcut by pressing Cmd + Opt + Esc to open the "force quit application" tool. From there, you can choose what you want to quit by clicking the "force quit" button. With this method, there is a risk of losing any unsaved work at the time of the freezing.

You can also reboot your Mac to unfreeze it, which is one of the easiest solutions, but that depends on how frozen your Mac is. This may be a challenge if you can't access your mouse cursor or any menus but if you just have an app frozen, then rebooting will be easier. To do this, you click the Apple icon on the top left of your screen and select the restart option and make sure that the "Reopen windows when logging back in" is unticked.

Powering down your Mac is another solution to help with unfreezing, although it isn't generally a good idea to forcefully turn your Mac off. This should be one of your last solutions if your mouse cursor is completely stuck and can't access menus. To do this, press and hold the power button, wait until your Mac shuts down, and then give it a few seconds before turning it back on.

You may also need to remove recently installed apps if your Mac keeps freezing right after you've installed them. Some ill-developed apps may cause your Mac to freeze up, so removing the offending apps should take care of the problem.

If your Mac keeps freezing, it's important to check your disk health. Computer hardware isn't meant to last forever and if your Mac keeps freezing, it could be a warning that your hard disk or SSD is failing. It could also be a result of data corruption, which is less catastrophic than the former. You can use the Disk Utility to run first aid and repair various problems affecting your Mac's disk.

Another solution to unfreezing your Mac would be by running a virus scan. Viruses and other types of malwares can slow down your Mac and freeze it. This is more of a preventative measure, and if you run a virus scan on a regular basis, then you can prevent your Mac from freezing.

Problem with Sound

This is a common issue and the first thing you need to do is ensure that your headphones or speakers are working and properly plugged in. If that doesn't solve it, here are some other ways you can go about it.

You'll need to check for internal and external issues.

How to Check for Internal Sound Issues

One of the ways to fix an internal sound issue is by going to the sound setting. If you are having an issue with the sound output, select "System Preferences" which is under the Apple menu, and click on "Sound" and that will lead you to the "Output." If the mute box is ticked, uncheck the box.

Apple Menu > System Preferences > Sound > Output

You should check if the sound works on other apps to confirm whether or not this problem is tied to a particular application. For example, if you are planning to facetime your grandkids but there is a sound issue, you can check to confirm if the other applications have functioning sounds, and if that is the case, then check the audio settings on the right volume bar to make sure they are on.

A malware or a virus can affect your sound and you need to look into your Mac's performance to ensure that is not the case. If it is indeed the case, you'll need to use a malware scanner to detect and exterminate the malware that may have spread across the system.

Updating your operating system is important as an older version of the OS can result in all sorts of malfunctions. You need to check and confirm that your Mac is running the newest version of the operating system; to do this, click on software update under System Preferences. If your Mac needs a system update, you will find a button to update.

How to Check for External Sound Issues

Check the connected Bluetooth device to ensure that they are actually turned on and connected. To fix this, go to Bluetooth under System Preferences, and check to see if it's turned on. Sometimes a device may fail to pair off automatically, and if that is the case, you can click on the "pair" button next to the device you wish to pair with.

In case you are playing something on your browser and it's muted, you should first check the settings of the browser you are using to ensure that the sound is turned on. If not, click on the menu in the top right corner of the window and select "Settings" then click on "Privacy and Security." On there you will find "Site settings" and if you scroll down, you'll see "Additional content settings" which will direct you to the sound.

Another way to fix your Mac's external sound issue is by troubleshooting external speakers. If you are using an external speaker, you need to ensure they are properly connected to the computer and that the audio port itself is clean from dust. If the cable is properly connected but there's still an issue, click on "System Preferences" and then select "Sound." Under sound, you will be able to access "Output" and here, you need to choose your external speakers as the output device. If you don't see that option, try unplugging and plugging the USB portal, but if it's connected via an audio port, then you'll receive a pop-up menu titled "Use Audio Port for..." and click on "Sound output."

Slow Performance

There are many reasons why your Mac would be running slowly, but some of the common ones include running low on RAM, overheated Mac, installing too many extensions on your browser, having too many files on your desktop, having too many browser tabs open, some apps storing too many log files and caches, malware on your Mac, and having a computer that is too old to support modern software.

You should check if any of the reasons listed above are the reasons your Mac is running slowly and work to fix it by using antivirus apps to remove malware or closing some of the tabs you have open in your browser. If you cannot find the cause to eliminate, then it's important to contact Apple customer support for assistance.

Running Out of Space

Macs can easily run out of storage space if you download multiple content on your computer. If you have idle apps you downloaded but don't use, you can delete them to clear up space or clear caches and log files. You can also erase old email attachments to clear up space if you are running out.

PART TWO: MAIN FEATURES OF MAC OS VENTURA

Overview

Everything we have discussed in the first part of the book sounds great on its own, so the question you may have is, what use is a system update? What else could Apple really do to make the Mac better than it already is?

Well, that's the thing about technology, there is always something that can be done to make it better than before. Although many fail to see the use of a new update when the older macOS setup runs just fine, it's worth noting that macOS updates have been consistently reliable over the years.

Apple's operating system has evolved over the last two decades and has worked to introduce new and unique features with every update. The first version of macOS was introduced to the market on the 24th of March, 2001. The macOS X, was made available to the public and it was pitched as an item that would improve computer use, and it has changed tremendously since.

The 13th and latest version of the operating system is the macOS Ventura, which was launched on October 24, 2022. This version was designed for contemporary desktop computers and Mac laptops, and the enhancements within this new release assist Mac users in core tasks' improvement. macOS Ventura is viewed as a significant update, and rightfully so. It introduces new experiences to Mac users by adding new multitasking features, updated capabilities, and an overhaul of multiple apps.

Some of the features of macOS Ventura are the Stage Manager for organizing apps and windows, Continuity Camera, updates to Safari and Mail, Undo Send, edit and mark messages as Unread, and more. We are going to discuss these features in detail and the ways in which they influence other applications.

In this portion of the book, we are going to discuss how macOS has improved the function of the Mac as discussed in the first part. We are also going to look into how you can install the operating system onto your Mac and whether or not it's compatible with your computer.

Most importantly, we are going to look into all the ways you can use this update to your advantage and ease the means by which you navigate.

How to Upgrade to macOS Ventura

macOS Ventura is assured to make things better than they already were, and in order to take full advantage of what your Mac has to offer, you need to get this update. Listed below are ways in which you can go about this.

Compatibility

The first thing you need to do is check whether or not macOS Ventura is compatible with your computer. There is a belief that as time progresses and older intel-based systems become outdated, it's going to be harder for Apple developers to accommodate older hardware and enable older Macs to run the newer versions of the operating system.

However, for this upgrade, there are many Macs, including the older models, that are compatible with the 13th macOS, macOS Ventura.

There are several tools available to help you identify the model of your Mac. One of the ways to go about this is by going to your "Apple Menu" which is in the upper left corner of your screen and selecting "About this Mac." You can also learn about the model in the system information app.

Apple Menu > About this Mac

In case you don't have your Mac with you or for whatever reason cannot start it, then you can learn the model by using the serial number on the original packaging or printed underneath your Mac, near the regulatory markings, and then entering the serial number on *check coverage page* or *Tech specs page.*

Once you have your model, use it to match with the Macs listed below to see if it is compatible with macOS Ventura.

MacBook Pro

MacBook Pro (13-inch, 2017, Two Thunderbolt 3 ports)

MacBook Pro (13-inch, 2017, Four Thunderbolt 3 ports)

MacBook Pro (15-inch, 2017)

MacBook Pro (13-inch, 2018, Four Thunderbolt 3 ports)

MacBook Pro (15-inch, 2018)

MacBook Pro (13-inch, 2019, Four Thunderbolt 3 ports)

MacBook Pro (15-inch, 2019)

MacBook Pro (13-inch, 2019, Two Thunderbolt 3 ports)

MacBook Pro (16-inch, 2019)

MacBook Pro (13-inch, 2020, Four Thunderbolt 3 ports)

MacBook Pro (13-inch, 2020, Two Thunderbolt 3 ports)

MacBook Pro (13-inch, M1, 2020)

MacBook Pro (14-inch, 2021)

MacBook Pro (16-inch, 2021)

MacBook Pro (13-inch, M2, 2022)

MacBook Air

MacBook Air (Retina, 13-inch, 2018)

MacBook Air (Retina, 13-inch, 2019)

MacBook Air (Retina, 13-inch, 2020)

MacBook Air (M1, 2020)

MacBook Air (M2, 2022)

MacBook

MacBook (Retina, 12-inch, 2017)

iMac Pro

iMac Pro (2017)

iMac

iMac (21.5-inch, 2017)

iMac Retina 4K (21.5-inch, 2017)

iMac Retina 5K (27-inch, 2017)

iMac Retina 4K (21.5-inch, 2019)

iMac Retina 5K (27-inch, 2019)

iMac Retina 5K (27-inch, 2020)

iMac M1 (24-inch, 2021)

Mac mini

Mac mini (2018)

Mac mini M1 (2020)

Mac Studio

Mac Studio (2022)

Mac Pro

Mac Pro (2019)

Backup Your Mac

It is very important to backup your Mac before installing new software, and this is to ensure you are able to restore your entire drive and also recover the previous version of a corrupted file. A program file or even data can be altered accidentally during the software update and backing it up will help recover it.

You should back up your Mac with Time Machine, which is a built-in feature of your Mac. It is built to automatically back up your personal data and it allows you to recover previous versions of files you can't presently access for whatever reason.

You can also opt to connect an external storage device such as a USB drive or Thunderbolt drive to your Mac to use for backups. However, you need to use the external storage device only as your Time Machine backup disk and it should have at least twice the storage volume you're backing. If the storage device does not have enough space to contain a complete backup, then Time Machine will let you know.

How to Use a Storage Device to Backup Your Data

Your Mac may ask if you want the Time Machine backups to be stored in the external storage device. However, if that does not happen then you can follow these steps. Depending on the macOS you are using, the process is going to vary.

First, click on the Apple Menu and then "System Preferences" to access Time Machine.

If you are backing up your data in macOS Ventura, you are going to have to click on the Apple Menu then to "System Settings" and then click "General" in the sidebar to access Time Machine.

Apple Menu > System Settings > General > Time Machine

Secondly, if the storage device you intend to use contains Time Machine backups from another Mac, you have the option to either claim the existing backups and make them a part of your Mac or start a new backup instead.

Once you've selected your storage device in the Time Machine settings, the backup process automatically begins making periodic backups. However, if you would rather backup manually and not wait for the next automatic backup, you can choose "Backup Now" from the Time Machine Menu.

Time Machine makes hourly backups and once it is full, then the oldest backups are deleted to make space for the new ones. If you want to adjust the backup frequency, open Time Machine Settings, and click "Options" then "Backup frequency" to choose a setting you want.

If you want to exclude an item from backups, then open Time Machine settings, click "Options" and then click the add (+) button to add an item to be excluded.

To check the status of your backup, you can use the Time Machine menu and you'll be able to view the date and time of the latest backup.

Free Up Storage Space on Your Mac

If your Mac startup disk is almost full, then you might not have enough space to download or install the new update. You can check how much space is available to accommodate additional files and free up your storage space.

One of the ways to go about this is by optimizing your storage by using iCloud to make storage space available. This helps free up space and you can use its in-built utilities to delete any items that are taking up space. We are going to discuss later how you can use iCloud to achieve this.

You can move files to an external drive for storage if you don't want to delete them. Some files such as photos and videos do happen to take up a lot of space and if you don't delete them, then moving them to external storage is a better solution for freeing up your computer's storage space.

If you delete a file to clear the space, you need to make sure you empty Trash as its space doesn't become available until it's cleared from there.

Update macOS on Your Mac

Once you're sure that your computer is compatible with macOS Ventura, you've backed up your data, and there is adequate space, then the last step is updating your operating system.

There are two ways of going about this. The first is by using Software Update and the second is by downloading it. While installing the update, you will be able to view the progress bar on the screen and your Mac will restart, so do not close the lid or put your Mac to sleep mode.

Use Software Update

This is the first way you can update your Mac and it's admittedly the easiest. It also requires less space to download and install the newest upgrade.

To go about this, you need to click the "Apple Menu" in the corner of your screen and then choose, "System Settings." Next, click "General" in the sidebar and then click "Software Update" on the right.

Apple Menu > System Settings > General > Software Update

If your Mac does not have those settings, click the "Apple Menu," choose "System Preferences" and then click "Software update."

Apple Menu > System Preferences > Software Update

Under software update, you will find the "Update now" button. Click it to install the update.

You may be asked to enter your administration password, so proceed as prompted, and during the installation, your Mac will restart and you will be able to see a progress bar and blank screen several times, so don't panic if you do. Don't try to shut down your computer or unplug it from the power source.

In case you don't see the software update in the System Preferences or System Settings, you can search for it in the corner of the window, but if you still can't access it, then you head over to the next method, which is downloading it from the App Store.

If you don't have enough storage space, then you will receive a message and the installation will not go through. In addition to having enough storage space, you need to check your internet connection to ensure the installer is able to get information specific to your Mac.

Use App Store or Browser

Your Mac is going to need more storage if you adopt this method, but if you can't use the software update, then this is another way to go about installing macOS Ventura.

To go about this, first, click the link to open the App Store for macOS Ventura and then click the "Get" button to begin downloading the macOS installer to your application folder.

Once the download is complete, the installer will open automatically. Follow the instructions on the screen to install macOS Ventura.

If you are experiencing difficulty in getting the link to work, try accessing it using Safari.

This particular option is going to need a lot more space than the first, so you need to check if you have enough storage space and use the methods we've listed above to clear up your storage.

If macOS Ventura is not compatible with your Mac, then the App Store will prevent you from downloading it and the installer will let you know by dimming the "Get" button or by stating that the requested version of macOS is unavailable.

Stage Manager

The Stage Manager in Mac is a window and app organization system that helps with clutter by putting the app you are using at the center and your recent apps in a column on the left of your screen.

This is considered to be one of the best new features in the macOS Ventura as it introduces all the new ways in which you can multitask and work with several apps and files at once. This means you can put the app you're currently using at the front and center of the desktop while the other apps are tucked at the side for quick access when you need to use them. The apps tucked to the side remain invisible but will pop up when you hover your cursor in that general direction. Essentially, it makes it easy to view information from multiple applications and switch between apps with ease and speed.

There is already an app, Mission Control, that helps with windows where you can have them all open at once, but it doesn't necessarily have the same organization elements the Stage Manager presents. Mission Control is good and has been sufficient in providing a bird's eye view to all open windows, desktop spaces, and the apps in full screen or split view. However, it's nothing compared to the Stage Manager, which covers all the organizational elements missing in Mission Control.

In Stage Manager, windows are sorted by individual apps as thumbnails, and by clicking the thumbnails, the window opens on the screen; so, for instance, if you have multiple windows of an app open, they will appear as stacked thumbnails, so you'll keep clicking until the window you want appears.

It also allows you to create groups of windows that go together with your workflow; if, for instance, you are doing some research on a farming tool to send to your son-in-law, you can have Pages, Safari, iMessage, and Notes apps open, and you can group them to ease your access. To go about this, you drag each thumbnail to the center of the screen and once they are all on the screen, click on one of the thumbnails and the Stage Manager will automatically create the group. When you click the group thumbnail, all the apps you have saved there will appear on the screen.

This system needs a little patience to adjust to, but it's a huge improvement over Mission Control because it reduces the time you spend hunting for a window when all you need is to turn to the left side of your screen to access it. It is particularly handy when you are focused on big projects when minimizing windows over and over to use them proves to be a chore.

In case you find this new feature too complicated for you, then you should know that it's optional. You can choose to enable and disable it in the Control Center and use it only when it suits you. It's worth giving a try if you intend to use multiple applications simultaneously or transfer information between Apps.

How to Use Stage Manager in macOS Ventura

Using Stage Manager may seem confusing at first and you may be tempted to get rid of it. However, it just requires a little patience and once you understand how to make use of it, then everything becomes easier for you.

When you enable Stage Manager, if you have an open window, then it will remain on the screen. When you open another application, your current window will minimize and move to the side of your screen.

If you want to pair applications into a group, you will drag the applications you want to use from the left side of the screen to the center, and when you open a new application, the windows will move to the side and be grouped together. Now, whenever you want to use an application, you will click on the group and bring them forward and pick up where you left off.

After you are done using the apps and would like to clear your desktop of windows, then you can go about this by clicking Cmd + M or using the minus button in windows to minimize the applications.

To clear the windows on the side of Stage Manager, press Cmd + H when the application is on your desktop, and to bring the window back up click on the app icon in your dock.

How to Enable Stage Manager in macOS Ventura

Stage Manager is optional and if you want to use it, there are simple steps you can go about to enable it, and you can follow the same to disable it if you change your mind.

To enable Stage Manager in macOS Ventura, you'll have to access it through the Control Center. First, open the menu bar to access the Control Center icon, then click on it to get to the Stage Manager. Click "Turn on Stage Manager" to enable the feature.

Alternatively, you can enable Stage Manager in System Settings. Open System Settings, click on "Desktop and Dock" and scroll down to "Stage Manager." The settings menu gives you the option to customize Stage Manager's interface and you can choose to show more than just recent applications but also include other items such as folders.

Apple Menu > System Settings > Desktop & Dock > Stage Manager

Continuity Camera

This is another new feature that was introduced in the macOS Ventura. So, what does it do?

As much as Mac has decent webcams, Continuity Camera allows your Mac to take advantage of the superior camera quality of your iPhone by connecting the two devices. You can connect your iPhone to your Mac wirelessly and also automatically by positioning your iPhone on top of the Mac using a stand.

Once connected, Continuity Camera works as an external webcam and allows you to select camera-leveraging utilities such as Facetime.

This feature allows you to use your iPhone's rear camera as an alternative to your Mac's webcam, but it goes beyond that. You can use this connection when you want to insert photos or scan documents.

We are going to discuss the functions of this feature and how to go about them.

System Requirements for Continuity Camera

To be able to use Continuity Camera, you are going to need a few things:

First, you need to ensure that your Mac is running macOS Ventura.

Your iPhone or iPad must be on iOS 16 or later.

Your iPhone and Mac both need to be signed in to the same Apple ID with a two-factor authentication enabled.

You also need to make sure that Bluetooth and Wi-Fi on both devices are enabled.

Lastly, an iPhone mount or stand to place on top of your Mac's screen.

How to Use Your iPhone as the FaceTime Camera

You can use your iPhone as the main camera during a Facetime call on your Mac, but you're going to need to purchase a stand to place on top of your Mac.

When you have everything, you need, bring the two devices close and your Mac will automatically switch to your iPhone's camera input.

Click on the "Control Center" and then "Video effects" and select which effect you want to use during your call.

It also supports Center Stage, which pans to keep you in frame and allows your camera to follow you or pinpoint the main subject currently speaking, and Portrait Mode, which blurs the background around the subject.

How to Use Desk View with Your iPhone and Mac

An additional feature is the "Desk View," which does exactly as it suggests. It shows your desk and face at the same time. It mimics an overhead camera and you don't need to adjust your phone when using this feature.

To use it, open the Control Center and click "Video Effects." Select "Desk View" and another window will open. Align it with how you want Desk View to be set, and when everything is to your liking, click "Start Desk View."

To disconnect your iPhone as the main camera, you can take your iPhone off your Mac and choose to either "pause" or "disconnect" from your iPhone.

New App Features

Messages

The Messages app did not get major changes in terms of its design. However, there are some features that have been introduced to the app that may prove helpful. One of the things most Mac users have been anticipating for years is the edit option. This is an option that allows iMessage to be edited up to 15 minutes after it has been sent or unsend it up to 2 minutes after it's delivered.

We've all had those instances where we've sent the wrong message or mistakenly sent it to the wrong person. You're probably planning a surprise visit to see your kids and you happen to spoil the surprise with a simple message. Well, macOS Ventura introduces a feature that allows you to edit or, better yet, unsend that message.

It is important to note that editing and unsending messages do not work with SMS. It can only be done with "blue bubble," and it requires all parties to have either macOS Ventura or iOS 16 installed.

You also have the option to mark messages as unread if you don't have time to respond to them. If you receive a message and you don't want to deal with it right away, you can easily mark it as unread so that you don't forget to respond when it's convenient to do so.

In case you accidentally delete a message, you have the option to recover it for up to 30 days after deletion. If you want to access the recently deleted messages, you will find them in the filtered section of the Messages app.

A major update to Messages is in its role having been modified to work with SharePlay. SharePlay allows you to join synchronized activities like playing games, watching movies, listening to music, using apps, and more with family or friends. With the new update, you can do all this whilst chatting with your family using Messages or on FaceTime.

Safari

With the previous macOS, the Tab Groups feature was introduced to Safari. This is a feature that allows you to group tabs and keep related pages together in a single organized workspace. With macOS Ventura, this feature can now be shared: A group of people can share a set of tabs and everyone can make adjustments and view the updates made to the tabs.

In macOS Ventura, tabbed groups have their own start pages, so each tab has its own customized background image and favorites. You can also include pinned tabs in groups, as well.

Additional changes to the app can also be found in the new web extension that syncs across all devices and the Application Programming Interface (API) for developers to create new kinds of Safari extensions. The website settings of pages such as Zoom and automatic reader view will also be able to sync across all devices.

There is also added support for opt-in notifications from Safari pages on macOS and web page translation. Languages such as Turkish, Thai, Korean, Arabic, Polish, Dutch, Indonesian, and text images on the web can be translated using live text.

macOS Ventura allows you to manage your Wi-Fi passwords in Network Preferences, where you can reference and share passwords or delete old ones. You also can edit strong passwords to adjust for site-specific requirements following suggestions made by Safari.

How to Share Tab Groups

As previously discussed, macOS allows you to share Tab Groups in Safari with your family, friends, and colleagues. The Tag Group feature was introduced in macOS Monterey and it was intended to ease the task of preserving and organizing open tabs in Safari.

It's easy to collect and save related webpages in a tab, and in macOS Ventura, you can share and allow multiple people to contribute to the tab. If you are collaborating on a project with your family or friends, then sharing tabs makes it easier to contribute to the project and complete the task. So, instead of constantly sharing links to webpages, anyone can just access the webpage and make their own contribution on the shared tab and it will be updated immediately.

If you want to share an open tab in Safari, then you'll need to access Safari's sidebar by clicking the "Show sidebar" button. Next, click the vertical ellipsis button (three encircled dots) next to the Tab Group you want to share, and select "Share Tab Group" from the menu. From there, you are going to choose the sharing method from the share sheet menu.

You can choose to send an invite via Mail or Messages, which will open the associated app with a link to the Tab Group. If you want to check who has access to the Tab Group, then you can click the user profile icon in the Tab Overview screen, which you will find under the same ellipsis button.

Mail

There are quite a number of changes you will find in the mail app in macOS Ventura. For one, the tools for unsending emails have been adjusted in a way in which you can unsend an email in 10 seconds before it reaches the recipient. This is feature is similar to the Message app, but unlike that feature, the mail does not leave a message behind to indicate that you unsent the email.

You also have the option to schedule an email to be sent in the future and a "Remind me option" that acts to remind you to reply to an email if you cannot respond right away. You'll also receive notifications if you forget to include important parts of your email message like recipient and attachments.

macOS has also made the search in the Mail app faster and with better accuracy than before by having the app anticipate what you want to search and then providing a wider view of content when you start the search. The search will also automatically correct any typos and will search for synonyms to ease access. The Mail app has also been modified to support links to weblinks and other information to give more context to your emails.

You can also move a sent email message to the top of your inbox, making it easier to access it whenever you need and then quickly send a follow-up. Say you don't receive a response to the email you sent, moving an email to the top makes it easier for you to follow up on the anticipated mail and the email exchange between you and the recipient.

How to Undo Send in Apple Mail

For whatever reason, if you regret sending an email message immediately after you press Send, you can make sure it doesn't arrive at its intended destination, but you only have 10 seconds to do so, after which the message cannot be unsent.

The "Undo Send" option briefly appears at the bottom of the sidebar immediately after you've sent the email. It will show for a few seconds before disappearing, so you need to act quickly to unsend it. If you are worried that 10 seconds is just plain unreasonable, well, then you can adjust the interval settings to 20 or even 30 seconds, giving you a little more time.

To adjust the settings, open your mail app and select "Mail" then "Settings" from the menu bar. Next, select the "Composing Tab" in the settings window, and under "Sending" click the dropdown menu next to "Undo Send delay" and select one of the options: "30 seconds," "20 seconds," "10 seconds," and "off." Choose the setting you prefer to make and save the changes, and your Undo Send delay option will come into effect immediately.

Mail > Settings > Composing Tab > Sending > Undo Send delay

How to Use Scheduled Send in Apple Mail

One of the features added to the macOS Ventura is the new Scheduled Send feature. The previous versions of macOS lacked some of the mail app features that are quite basic to rival apps, but Ventura has brought about the modification to make the app more efficient.

The scheduled send does exactly that. It sends emails at a scheduled time and this allows you to compose a message in the mail and then set a time and date in the future at the point you want the mail to be sent. So basically, you can simply type emails in advance and if you don't want to send them immediately, then it'll happen automatically when you set the time.

So, how do you go about this?

You first open the Mail app and click the "Compose new message" button where you will enter your intended recipients, add a subject title, and compose your email. Once you are done with your email, click the downward chevron (guillemet symbol) that is next to the Send icon. From the dropdown, you will get options such as "Send now," "Send tomorrow," and "Send later," and clicking the last option will bring you a clock and calendar for you to set the specific time and date you want your email to be sent. Once you've made your selection, then you are going to click "Schedule."

Once you have done all that, there is no need to worry as your email will be sent at the scheduled date and time.

How to Receive Reminders in Apple Mail

One of the major improvements in macOS Ventura lies in its ability to send reminders to respond to specific email messages in your inbox. You've probably had a time or two when you've read an email and pushed it aside to reply to it later but then you forget all about it until it was too late. The reminder button helps with this inconvenience as you don't have to worry about forgetfulness when macOS Ventura is there to worry for you.

First, you need to set it up, and to go about this, open your Apple Mail and right-click a message in your inbox and you will see the "Remind me" option from the contextual menu. From the submenu, you'll be able to see "Remind me in 1 hour," "Remind me tonight," "Remind me tomorrow," or "Remind me later."

Just like with the scheduled reply feature, if you select "Remind me later," a dialogue will appear for you to select the time and date you want to receive the reminder. Once you've selected the time and date, click, "Schedule."

Once you have completed this, you will receive a reminder about the specific email at the set time, but if you later decide that you don't want to be reminded about the message, choose "Remind me later" and then select "Clear Reminder" from the contextual menu.

FaceTime

This is another app that has seen some changes in the macOS Ventura. FaceTime calls can now be accepted on the iPhone or iPad before being transferred to the Mac and vice versa. When you hand off a call, the connected handset transitions to the new device seamlessly.

macOS Ventura also supports a new feature that allows you to collaborate with others in Files, Safari, Reminders, Keynote, The Finder, Pages, and even third-party apps. What this means is you can start a Facetime call in these apps with your collaborators and video chat as you discuss what you are working on—and all that with a simple click.

With macOS Ventura, there is live caption where you can see automatically transcribe dialogue in your Facetime videos, and with the speaker attribution, you are able to easily tell who is speaking during the call.

Photos

Say you have a number of duplicate images in your photo library. First of all, they are taking up space and you might need to get rid of them to clear it up. However, macOS introduced a feature that detects duplicate images and merges them together. This will deal with the stress of trying to figure out what to delete from your library.

The people album can also be sorted alphabetically and additionally, edits made to a single photo can be copy pasted onto another photo. What this means is if you make edits to a photo, you don't have to repeat the entire process from scratch, you can simply copy the edits onto another image.

In macOS Ventura, there is also a new photo picker for importing photos and videos into the system from the library, and for people who do not like the memories and featured photos selection, you can easily disable the features.

"This Day in History" and "Children playing" are the new memory types and Apple Music subscribers can also add millions of songs to their memories from the Apple Music Library to listen to on their devices. Additionally, while a video is playing in Memory, you can restart the video and play it from the beginning with the music still playing.

With the macOS Ventura, there is also the option to lock the hidden and recently deleted albums in the photos to be accessed using a login password or Touch ID.

How to Find, Merge and Delete Duplicate Photos in macOS

Tracking down duplicates in the photo library is a feature that was absent before macOS Ventura. If one wanted to get rid of the duplicates, they would have to get a third-party app, but all that has been simplified in the new macOS.

In macOS Ventura, the photo app automatically detects any duplicates in your photo library and collates them together for you to decide what to do with them. Apple has added a new Duplicates album in the gallery app, which you can find in the photo's sidebar. However, the album only appears when you have duplicate images in your photo library.

When you open the duplicate album, you will find the duplicates listed in chronological order with a "Merge" option listed beside each set. You can choose to merge the images by clicking the "Merge" button and this feature will allow you to keep the highest detail and important metadata, thus giving you the best possible image. You will get the best single image from a combination of the best details from the photos you choose to merge.

The merge is not restricted to just two photos as you can merge several sets of duplicates in your photo album; for this, you are going to select the duplicates you want to merge by clicking them with your cursor while holding the Cmd key. You could also select all the images by clicking on one, then choosing "Edit" and then "Select All" from the menu bar.

Once you have selected all the images you want to duplicate, click the "Merge" button at the top right of the window.

You can delete selected duplicates by right-clicking one and choosing the photos to delete from the contextual menu.

When you are done merging or deleting the duplicates, then the duplicates album will disappear and only show up again when your Mac detects other duplicates in your photo album.

Clock

This is new to Mac. The clock app has been present on the iPad and the iPhone but is now present on the Mac, as well, and it enables seamless continuity between the devices. The app supports Siri integration for setting alarms, timers, and asking for the time in another city. It also enables you to tell the local time in different time zones around the world and you can set an alarm with a custom alert sound accordingly.

The Clock app's functionality can be extended with shortcuts. You can easily access it from the menu bar, or the Finder. You can also ask Siri without having to access the app.

Weather

The Weather app is another addition to the Mac, and although it has the same design as the Weather app on the iPhone and iPad, it has notable differences as the version on Mac has been optimized for a larger display. For starters, it has immersive animations, higher-detailed maps, and clickable forecast modules.

This app has features present in the iOS apps such as the animated weather background that changes based on the current weather, alerts on severe weather, air quality monitoring, forecast, and weather maps.

You can monitor the air quality by use of a color-coded scale that displays the quality level and the category in which it falls. So, if the air quality is better or worse than the previous day, then you will be able to view it on the map and get related health recommendations, pollutant breakdown, and more information relating to it.

In addition to that, you are able to view the weather forecast in a smart layout that adjusts to the current conditions. The weather maps aid in showing precipitation, temperature, and air quality to help plan healthier immersion. The app reveals a deeper set of data such as hourly temperature and precipitation over the next ten days.

Home

The Home app has a new design that makes it simpler to navigate, view, organize, and control all smart home accessories. The improvements made to the underlying framework work to enhance a smart home's devices' performances, thus making them more efficient and reliable.

With the updates in macOS Ventura, there are redesigned home tabs that make it possible to view your entire home with a single glance. The rooms and favorite accessories have all been integrated into the app's main tabs, giving you easier access to the accessories you use the most.

There is a selection of categories available at the top of the app and it works to organize accessories into Climate, Light, Security, Speakers, TVs, Water, and more. This makes it easy and fast to get to the accessory you are looking for. The new sidebar layout makes it simpler to access the accessories by room along with detailed status information.

The Home app in macOS Ventura supports Matter. Matter is a new smart home connectivity standard designed to enable compatible accessories from Apple, Google, Samsung, and other smart home manufacturers to work seamlessly across all platforms (cross-platform functionality). This will allow you to choose from even more compatible smart home accessories and control them with the Home app.

Maps

The Maps app in macOS Ventura supports multi-stop routing, which automatically syncs with your iPhone when you are ready to leave. So, what this does is help you plan out a trip with multiple stops and you can also view and calculate how much your journey will cost you with transit fares.

Notes

The new filters introduced in macOS Ventura ensure that Notes are automatically organized in smart folders. There are rules available for Date created, Date modified, Mentions, Shared, Attachments, Checklists, Folders, Quick Notes, Locked Notes, and Pinned Notes.

The new layout has been designed in a certain way so that notes are grouped chronologically by categories like "Today" and "Yesterday" for easy reference, plus you can also share notes and anyone with the link can join.

You also have the option to encrypt your notes end-to-end with Mac's login password. With macOS Ventura, there is a nice balance in having means by which you can share a link to collaborate with other people to share your notes and encrypting locked notes to limit their access.

Reminders

There are quite a number of features introduced to the Reminders app in macOS Ventura and one of them is pinned lists. This feature allows you to pin favorite lists for quick access.

Lists can also be saved as templates to make it easy to reuse them for routines, packing lists, and more. The templates can be published and shared using a link and you can easily download templates other people have shared and used in your Reminders app.

There is also the Completed Smart Lists feature that enables you to view all completed reminders in one place with all their information, like time of completion.

The Scheduled Lists feature has new months and week groups that assist with long-term organization. The time and date-based grouping makes it easy to access and add reminders and to help with diving into your day, the Today's lists feature is now grouped by "Morning," "Afternoon," and "Tonight."

You can also click on a list group for a combined view of the lists and reminders it contains.

macOS Ventura also enables richer notes, in that, when adding notes to your reminders, you can create bullets, underline, bold, or even strike through the text. This will make it easier to organize your reminders in a neater manner.

There is also a Notification in shared lists where you receive an alert for any tasks added or completed in shared lists.

In addition to all the new features, this new update to the app lets you choose whether or not to filter any of the criteria selected in a Custom Smart List or the Tag Browser.

iCloud

There are quite a number of updates made to iCloud to improve it. One of the features added to iCloud is the Shared Photo Library, which makes it easier to not only share photos with your family members but the feature also gives them access to add, edit, favorite, caption, and delete shared photos, as well. This feature allows you to share an iCloud Photo Library with up to five people, but there are smart setup rules that can be implemented to prevent accidentally sharing photos you would rather keep to yourself.

There are settings that allow you to share all past photos or photos from a specific date. Let's say for instance you attended one of your kids' graduation parties. There are going to be a lot of photos taken with friends and family and you may want to share them. Of course, you want to share the photos from the graduation and not the ones from before or after. In this case, you opt to share photos from that specific date.

Photos can also be added to the shared Library automatically but you have the option to share based on Bluetooth proximity. If you want to view the pictures you have shared and relive more complete memories, you can find them in Memories, Featured photos, or the photos widget.

System Settings

In macOS Ventura, "System Preferences" has been renamed "System Settings" but it's not just the name that has received a major change.

The previous macOS, macOS Monterey, used a multi-icon layout, but the new settings under macOS Ventura have adopted an iOS-like design with a sidebar that aggregates the different settings.

System Settings is meant to be easier to navigate with the sidebar as you don't have to swap through different settings panels. This makes it easy to quickly configure your device without having to drill into and out of views, and with more spaces in each setting pane, it becomes considerably easier to locate the settings you want with ease.

The sidebar is organized by categories that include Appearance, Control Center, and Desktop. Similar categories are grouped close together for consistency across iOS, iPadOS, and macOS.

The search on System Settings has also been improved to streamline your searches with just a couple of simple keywords. If you have no idea where to find a specific setting, you can easily type it in the search fields, which is at the top of the new sidebar.

You can now access and customize AirPods features in one place and when they are connected, the menu will appear at the top of settings.

Freeform App

Freeform is an app that provides a blank canvas for collaborative purposes. It helps you brainstorm with the use of text, images, lines, and shapes, and you can draw, make sticky notes, or even make lists. You can also collaborate with others on brainstorming on projects and more.

The freeform is a cross-platform app and it supports real-time collaborations, so, essentially, you can view other people's contributions to the project. The app uses the Messages app and FaceTime to aid in chatting with collaborators. Videos, audio, images, weblinks, PDFs, and other documents can all be added to the canvas and previewed without having to leave Freeform to open another app. Basically, you can add virtually any kind of file to the canvas without having to exit the app to access them.

The Freeform Canvas is great for aggregating important assets, diagramming new projects, and basically brainstorming on a board, so if you have a vague idea or a project you would like to explore but are yet to solidify, you can make use of the app to bring your abstract thought to shape with the tools available for you, and if you work with collaborators, you will be able to view their contributions and discuss the progress on FaceTime or Messages.

Spotlight

If you recall from previous sections, we mentioned that Spotlight is used to find apps, documents, emails, and other items on your Mac. With the macOS Ventura, there have been major improvements to the Spotlight app, adding support for Quick Look and Quick Actions.

You can preview files with Quick Look by pressing on the space bar on a result. With Quick Actions, Spotlight is allowed to do things such as start a timer, turn on a focus, run any shortcuts, find the name of a song with Shazam, and more.

With macOS Ventura, Spotlight now has an iOS-like search feature that brings together all the information you are looking for in one result. It provides rich results for sports, TV shows, businesses, movies, actors, musicians, and contacts.

Spotlight also uses the information from images in Photos, Notes, Messages, and Finder to enable searches by locations, scenes, or even things in the image like a piece of text or the presence of a dog.

Within the update is an integrated web search feature that allows you to conduct searches for images of people and even landmarks from the Spotlight interface.

Live Text

This is a feature designed to let the Mac recognize text in photos and images, and now with the macOS Ventura, it extends to video, as well. Text is interactive in paused videos making it easy to use functions like copy and paste, translate, and lookup text in any video you have on your Mac. This feature works in Safari, Quick Look, Photos, and in other apps, as well.

The Live Text feature also supports Quick Action as data detected in photos and videos is actionable with one click. There is a currency conversion feature and additionally, you can track flights and shipments, translate foreign languages, and more.

How to Use Live Text to Copy and Share Text in Video in macOS Ventura

The Live Text feature was first introduced to Mac users in the previous macOS build. This feature was able to automatically recognize text in images from Safari, Photos, Quick Look, Preview, and other sources. However, with macOS Ventura, that function now extends to video, as well. This update allows you to pause a video and interact with the text in the same way you would an image. The text on the paused video frame can be translated or you could even copy and paste it.

Live Text works in macOS Ventura in apps that support video and it is available in German, English, Spanish, French, and Japanese. So, how do you get it to work on a video?

First, you need to pause the video at the frame with the text you want displayed, then highlight what you want to copy by clicking and dragging a selection with your cursor. Next, right-click the highlighted text and you will see a menu of options including "Translate," "Copy," and "Share."

If you opt to copy the text, you'll need to switch to an app that supports text input, right-click on the cursor to bring up a popup, then select paste. Alternatively, you could press the Command (Cmd) + V shortcut to paste the text.

If you chose to translate the text, then its translation will automatically appear on the screen.

Visual Lookup

This is a picture-recognizing system that was introduced in macOS Monterey. The system can recognize well-known buildings, paintings, landmarks, different kinds of plants, and various breeds of animals, among others. In the latest macOS update, the feature can now recognize statues, birds, and insects.

With macOS Ventura, this feature lets you isolate the subject from an image by removing the background or by lifting it from the image with a click. The isolated image can be added to another or turned into a sticker.

This feature works in Photos, Screenshots, Safari, Quick Look, and other image-supporting apps.

Focus

Focus literally does as the name suggests: Focus on a task at hand by pausing or silencing distractive notifications.

The Focus feature in macOS Ventura has been improved by adding filter options. Boundaries have been created within Apple Apps, such as Mail, Calendar Messages, and Safari, that allow only parts of the apps to show. For example, in Safari, you can set a specific tab group to show, or in Calendar, you can choose to hide your personal Calendar and set it to show only a work Calendar.

You can have Focus turn on automatically while using a certain app. It can be scheduled to turn on at a specific time or location when it comes to the app.

This new update not only allows you to pause or silence notifications but you can also select apps or people you want to receive notifications from. The personalized setup allows you to be selective with the apps and people you receive notifications from by either silencing them or allowing them. When setting up Focus, you can make these adjustments to your Mac.

Passkeys

A passkey is an alternative means of signing in without needing to remember your password. So instead of a password, you use Face ID or Touch ID to identify yourself to an app or website account. You can sign in to your account if your Mac or Magic Keyboard has Touch ID.

Now with macOS Ventura and iOS 16, Apple is introducing this security feature as the modern and secure way of logging in online. Passkeys are way more secure than traditional passwords and protect users from attacks aimed at gaining access to their accounts.

macOS Ventura is introducing a new passkey feature that uses unique cryptographic key pairs for each account or website. One key is private and kept on the device and the other is public and stored on the website server. Devices with biometric authentication, Touch ID, or Face ID are used to authorize a passkey to authenticate the user to the website. The keys need to match to allow for a successful login because the second key is private and available only to the user. This way, it ensures it cannot be leaked, stolen, or phished.

Passkeys are synced across all your Apple devices through iCloud's Keychain, which is an end-to-end encryption with its own cryptographic keys and requires two-factor authentication for further protection.

The synchronization provides a backup in case an Apple device is lost, but if you happen to lose all your devices and the passkeys along with them, then Apple has an iCloud Keychain escrow in place to help recover your passkey information. Of course, there is a multi-step authentication process you need to go through to recover an iCloud Keychain, but you could also set up an account recovery contact.

All this may sound a little complicated on paper but in practice, passkeys are simple to master.

How to Create a Passkey for a New Account

The first thing you are going to do is sign up for a new account. However, in order to create a passkey, an iCloud Keychain must be set up on your Mac, and to go about it, you are going to choose "Apple Menu" and then select "System Settings."

From here, click your name at the top of the sidebar, and if you can't see your name, then click "Sign in with your Apple ID" to enter your Apple ID or create one if you don't have it already.

Next, you are going to click "iCloud" on the right and then turn on "Password & Keychain." You are then going to receive onscreen instructions to set up two-factor authentication. Before you can use iCloud Keychain, you need to set up your Mac to require a login password. This can be done in "Lock screen" under "System Settings."

Apple Menu > System Settings > Apple ID (Sign in with or Create Apple ID) > iCloud > Password & Keychain

When you sign up for a new account, you are going to enter your account name and then click to submit, and when you see the option to save a passkey for the account, you're going to have to choose how you prefer to sign in.

You could Touch ID on your Mac by placing your finger on the Touch ID sensor or scanning a QR code with your iPad or iPhone.

How to Sign in to an Account with a Passkey

On the account sign-in page, you are going to have to enter your account name and then click the account name field. On the list of suggestions, click your account and then you can proceed with one of the following choices.

Place your finger on the Touch ID sensor if you have Touch ID on your Mac.

If you have an iPad or iPhone, you can click "Other Options" and then click "Passkeys from nearby devices" and then click the QR code. The Bluetooth for both your iPad or iPhone and the Mac needs to be turned on.

The third option is to click "Other Options," select "Security key," and then follow the instructions on the screen.

How to Replace a Password with a Passkey

If you want to replace the password of an account and use a passkey instead, you are going to first sign in to the account with your password. The next step is to choose "System Settings" under the Apple Menu, then click "Passwords" in the sidebar.

Click the "info" button for the website and then click "Change Password" on the website.

Apple Menu > System Settings > Passwords > info

Accessibility

There are several accessibility options that are brought by macOS Ventura. Some of the new features are not new as they were previously on the iPhone but there are others that are completely novel.

Background sound is one of the features that is present in the iPhone but has now been made available for the Mac. You can minimize distraction or mask unwanted environmental noise by playing calming sounds such as the sound of rain or of the ocean.

You can also enlist help to move to the next level of a game through the Buddy Controller. This entails combining inputs from multiple game controllers into one so that a friend or even a care provider can help you get to the next level of the game.

We have previously discussed how the live captions generate transcriptions in real time and this comes in handy, especially for users who are deaf or have a hard time hearing. It also works in FaceTime where you automatically see the transcribed dialogue in your video calls. With the speaker attribution included, it makes it easier to follow a conversation and know who is speaking at a given time.

Voice control is another feature you can use on FaceTime. When the voice control is turned on, just use your voice and say, "Hang up," to end the call. It is important to note that the people on the call with you will hear you when you make this command.

Type to speak with live captions is another feature introduced to the Mac, and it works in a way where you can type a response and have it spoken aloud in real-time. You can use the Live Captions during FaceTime or with any app that facilitates video conferencing.

Voice Over is another feature in Mac and it has been made available in more than 20 additional languages and locales. You have the option to get an assistive feature from a selection of dozens of new voices. You can also discover formatting issues such as duplicate spaces through the text checker for Voice Over, before sharing the dictated text.

Additional Features

Game Center

The Game Center is an Apple service that allows users to play and challenge others in online games. This feature has seen some changes with macOS Ventura where the dashboard has been redesigned making it easier for the users to view their friends' play activity and achievements all in one spot.

It also integrates SharePlay making it so that you can play games with friends or family while on a FaceTime call.

Apple Pay

This is a mobile payment service by Apple Inc. supported on iPhone, iPad, Apple Watch, and Mac. It allows its users to make payments in person or on the web through their device.

With macOS Ventura, the payment sheet has been redesigned to make it easier to manage your information, add cards, and review details on purchases with an improved summary before completing your transaction.

Music

With macOS Ventura, there are new music notifications and recommendations that have been improved to help keep track of the artists you are more interested in.

News

The news now has a "My sports" section that includes all the info about leagues, your favorite players, and their teams. You can customize your feed to be able to view the latest stories, watch highlights, and receive notifications on scores, schedules, and the standings of the teams you support.

You can also get in-depth local coverage and access top newspapers with home pages and access your favorite channels or topics with a customized favorites group in the sidebar.

Siri

Siri has seen some updated designs with the macOS Ventura. These updates give more targeted results that aid in finding the information you are looking for. With the new software update, the results are more focused.

Stocks

The Stocks app supports the earning date for you to view when a company's upcoming report will take place and add it to your calendar.

You can also create multiple custom watchlists to help with organizing the tickers that you follow. You can use Group Symbols with any criteria you prefer, such as sector, ownership status, asset type, and more.

Security Updates

Security Updates can be applied to the Mac with the Rapid Security Response feature. With latest updates, you get important security improvements to your device that are applied automatically between normal updates.

The new security mode is set to provide extreme protection for users who face targeted threats to their digital security. It hardens the device's defenses and works to strictly limit certain functions in an effort to reduce attacks that could potentially be exploited by spyware.

PART THREE: BEST TIPS AND TRICKS FOR MAC OS VENTURA

Overview

In the previous chapters, we've discussed the features present in Mac and the updates the macOS Ventura has introduced to Mac users. From major updates like the ones you find in Stage Manager to the smallest details in the News feature, this system upgrade has a lot to offer. In this chapter, we are going to provide a quick summary of all that and look into all the tips and tricks you can adopt when it comes to navigating the new Operating System.

When macOS Ventura was introduced, it was met with mixed reactions. There were features that were loved and others not so much. Most of the features introduced are ones you can opt not to use. However, despite the work you feel goes into learning and adopting some of these features, it's important to try using them at least once before ruling them out. There are items we always think we can live without, but once we try them out, we find it hard to quit them, and the same applies to macOS Ventura's features.

In this chapter, we are also going to discuss some of the hidden macOS Ventura features that you need to check out for yourself. Additionally, we are going to look into some of the frequently asked questions and address any concerns you may have with adopting the new update.

Tips and Tricks for macOS Ventura

macOS Ventura brings updates for the Mac, such as Stage Manager, Passkeys, Camera Continuity, and many more. These are the features that everyone is talking about. They are very pronounced and major, but there are other slight features that hardly come up in discussions and those are the ones we are going to explore.

It takes a considerable amount of time to go through the entire Operating System in an attempt to discover the features the new update brings, so we'll do it for you. Some of the best tips and tricks lie in what we are not told but learn for ourselves. Here are some of the tips you can adopt to ease your access to the system.

View Weather Updates from Multiple Locations

The Weather app is one of the new system updates on Mac and it is an extended version of the apps on the iPhone and iPad. The Weather app is a huge deal especially because previous iterations of the macOS came with a Weather widget that only provided basic weather information.

This update doesn't receive the same attention as the others but it offers real-time information about various locations. It comes with multiple modules that feature information that could prove to be helpful.

It has the 10-day forecast which, as the name suggests, is a weather forecast summary for the next ten days that shows the chances of rain and the temperatures. It also shows the Air Quality with scales to relay when it's safe, acceptable, or increasingly unhealthy to go out.

The UV index is another module and it works to inform you of the levels of ultraviolet rays that are safe for you and those that carry a higher risk of harm after extended exposure.

The app also displays the time of sunrise and sunset and highlights the total daylight. The wind module indicates the speed and direction of the wind and you also get a display of the humidity and wind.

The "feels like" feature is one that indicates how the current temperature actually feels after evaluating factors like humidity and wind. The visibility feature covers miles and will let you know the total visibility of anything above six miles.

To use the weather app to get information and weather updates about various locations, you are going to search for the place you want in the search bar, select the place, and then click plus (+) button next to the search bar. You can access the location you have added from the sidebar in the top left corner.

FaceTime Handoff

Apple is known for coming up with upgrades that seamlessly transition activities between devices, so this new upgrade may not have come as a surprise to many. With the new system update, you can now continue a FaceTime call from one device to the other. Say you get a FaceTime call on your iPhone and you are near your Mac, you can transfer the call to your Mac and the transition is so seamless that there won't even be any interruptions. The same will apply to your Mac as you can transfer the call from your computer to your iPhone or iPad without any issues.

Password-protected Photos

Chances are you live with people who can access your Mac. If you have photos you would rather keep for yourself, then the good news is that macOS Ventura supports password protection for the Photo app. The password will not only protect the photos in your hidden album but also protect the recently deleted sections, and when you try to open them, you will be required to enter a password.

Duplicate Photos

Photos can take considerable disk space in your Mac's storage and one of the ways to create space is to get rid of some of the photos. This update creates a solution for when you need to create space by giving you options to deal with duplicates.

Apple has brought a section where you can view duplicates and decide whether to merge or delete them.

Lift a Subject from the Background

There are many features added to the Photos app. From password protection and duplicate photos to memories, the Photos app has seen major upgrades. However, the ability to copy a subject and paste it is one of the incredible features that doesn't receive enough attention.

If you want to copy a subject in Quick Looks, you first open the photo you want, right-click on it, and select the "copy subject" option. You are going to see highlights around the subject and you can post the subject anywhere you want.

It is important to note that the ability to copy subjects works on photos taken in portrait mode or in photos where the subject easily stands out as that helps the software detect it.

Collaborate on Notes

One of the most common features that have improved with macOS Ventura is the collaborative feature. With the new software update, you can easily collaborate with people on multiple apps, and while most people are more excited about being able to collaborate on apps like Safari in group tabs, not much stock is put in notes. However, this is the one place where you place abstract thoughts, and being able to collaborate with others on the same plane is a great experience.

To collaborate on notes, you are going to open the note you want to collaborate on and click the "Share" button and then select "collaborate." You also need to select "everyone can make changes" to manage permissions.

Schedule, Undo, and Set Reminders for Email

Apple put work into improving email with this new update. If you are a forgetful person then the reminders feature will come in handy, but that's not all. You can unsend an email within 10 seconds by clicking the "undo send" button from the bottom left corner and the best part is the recipient doesn't get to learn about it. You can also schedule emails to be sent at a time of convenience.

Suppose you need to send an email early in the morning but you don't want to wake up to compose it. You can compose the email at night and schedule it to be sent the next morning while you stay in bed.

Besides adding the schedule, undo, and set reminders features to the mail app, Apple has also improved the existing search features and you can still get your desired results even when you search with typos. They provide results and ask whether that was what you meant to search for.

Search Results from Images

Picture this, you saw a term but you don't exactly remember where you saw it, so you go to Spotlight and search for it. The results you get from your system will also contain images that contain the search term.

This is a great feature that does not get the same attention as the other updates. This feature is useful especially if you don't want to go through all the images searching for the text you want.

Passkeys

All the features that come with the system update are great and all, but none of them compare to passkeys. This is perhaps the best step Apple has taken in terms of protecting your data. The passkeys replace the traditional password and are more effective in their protective roles than the passwords.

Live Captions

The role of the live captions have now been extended in Mac. When turned on, it automatically generates transcriptions and you can view what is being said on the screen making it easier to follow along with the audio and video conversations. This applies to FaceTime, as well.

If you have hearing issues, then this is a great feature that helps you follow up with the live conversation, and the best part is that the transcripts will not appear in screenshots.

Dictation

Where Live Caption transcribes what is being said on the screen, Dictation on the other hand transcribes what you speak, meaning you can dictate and type simultaneously.

The best part about this feature is that it will insert commas, periods, and question marks where they are needed. If you want, you can add emojis via dictation, but you need to remember their correct name for that to happen. Either way, this is a great feature that doesn't receive the same amount of attention as the rest.

FAQ

Q. When will macOS Ventura be released?

A. The new macOS 13 Ventura was released on 24th October 2022.

Q. How much will it cost to get the update installed?

A. You can download the new Operating System from the Apple Mac's App Store for free.

Q. How do I install the update on multiple computers?

A1. You have two options to go about this. The first option is to download Ventura individually on each computer.

A2. The second option is to download the Ventura installer on one of the computers, quit the installer, and copy it to each computer's application folder that you want to install the Ventura on.

Q. Which Macs can I install the macOS Ventura on?

A. The following Macs are compatible with Ventura:

MacBook Pro (2017 or newer)

MacBook Air (2018 or newer)

MacBook (2017 or newer)

iMac Pro (2017 or newer)

iMac (2017 or newer)

Mac Pro (2019 or newer)

Mac Studio (2022 or newer)

Mac mini (2018 or newer)

You also need an Apple ID to be able to get Ventura from the Mac App Store.

Q. Which Mac do I have?

A. To check the model of your Mac, go to the Apple Menu > About this Mac > Overview tab, and then check for the computer name at the top of the line. For example, it may read "MacBook Air."

To view the model date version, go to the Apple Menu > About this Mac > Overview tab, and then check for the details after the model's name. For example, "Early 2017."

To be more specific, you can check your Mac's model identifier by clicking on the Apple Menu > About this Mac > More info, and the system profiler application will open, then select "Hardware" at the top left and check what it says for "model identifier."

Q. My Mac is compatible with the macOS Ventura but my internet connection is slow, will that be a problem?

A. No, this will not be a problem; however, you need to note that the Ventura installer is 12 GB in size and if you have slow internet, it will take a considerable amount of time to download.

Q. I don't have a permanent internet connection, will this be a problem?

A. Yes. To download macOS Ventura from the Mac App Store, you are going to need an internet connection.

Q. I have an Internet data cap in place and cannot download something that is 12 GB in size. What can I do?

A. It's important to note that Ventura will not be available on a USB thumb drive or optical disk, so you are going to have to use a different internet connection that does not have an internet access data cap.

You could alternatively go to an Apple Retail Store and install Ventura from their local server.

Q. Why can't I download Ventura from my current macOS?

A. It's important to first make sure that your Mac is compatible with Ventura. The next step is to make sure that you have adequate storage space to accommodate the large update.

Q. What are the new features in macOS Ventura?

A. The recommended features to note include the Passkeys, Message enhancements (with the edit, undo send, and recover deleted messages), Stage Manager, Continuity Camera that allows you to use your iPhone as your webcam, Clock app, Weather app, a redesigned System Settings, Redesigned Home app, iCloud Shared library, Gameplay SharePlay, and Enhanced Accessibility.

These are some of the common features but it is also important to note that not all the features will be available for all Mac models, Countries, or areas of residence.

Q. Does Ventura include Hypertext Preprocessor (PHP)?

A. No, the PHP utility has been removed. You can install it with Homebrew or alternatively, use a third-party software stack to install it.

Q. Does Ventura use Core Storage?

A. Yes. The Disk Utility gives you access to some of the Core Storage features and formatting.

Q. If I install macOS Ventura and find that I don't like it, can I easily downgrade back to an older version of macOS?

A. Yes. You can downgrade back to the previous macOS you were running but this will not be an easy process. However, it will be fairly easy to downgrade if your Mac originally came with the older version of macOS installed; this is because you can use the built-in macOS recovery tool to downgrade. Before you downgrade, you are going to need to first back up your data.

Q. Is updating to macOS Ventura worth it?

A. Updating to the latest software ensures you get the latest features but some can take a while to get adjusted to. If the latest features sound appealing to you, then upgrading to macOS 13 Ventura is a great idea, but if you are unwilling to adopt the new system this new update brings, then you can give yourself a little more time to get accustomed to the idea.

The good news is you can always go back to your older version if the new one does not appeal to you.

Printed in Great Britain
by Amazon

22936946R00044